Contents

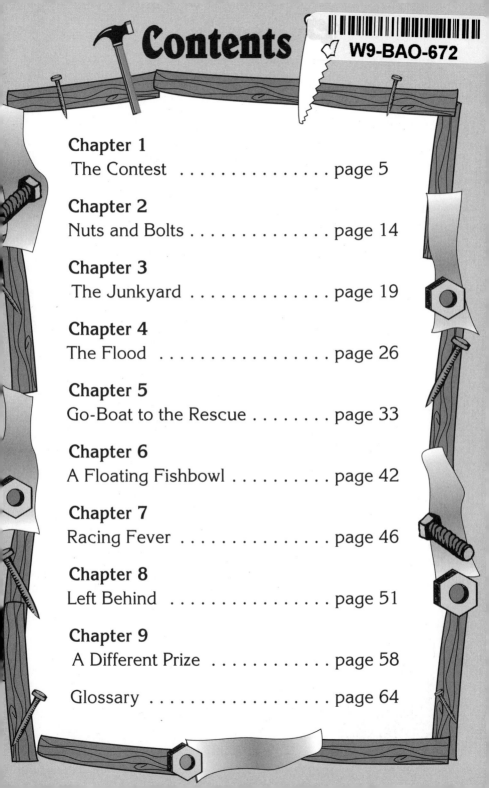

W9-BAO-672

For my brother Tom,
with hugs and kisses

The GO-BOAT

By Jane Vecchio
Illustrated by Thea Kliros

Modern Curriculum Press
Parsippany, New Jersey

Cover and book design by John Maddalone

Modern Curriculum Press
An imprint of Pearson Learning
299 Jefferson Road, P.O. Box 480
Parsippany, NJ 07054–0480

www.pearsonlearning.com

1-800-321-3106

ISBN 0-7652-2158-6

2 3 4 5 6 7 8 9 10 11   MA   07 06 05 04 03 02 01

The Contest

The meteorologist on television grinned and turned away from his weather map. "That's the weather for the next few days, sunny, but cold! Brrrrrr! Back to you, Bill!"

Wendy Asato sat on the couch and yawned. The TV news was so boring that she was ready to turn it off. Nothing very interesting seemed to be going on in her hometown of River City.

"Now a story about a special contest for River City's young people," said the announcer.

Wendy perked up. She was a young person who lived in River City. She also loved entering contests. Maybe this news story would be interesting.

"Calling all inventors," the reporter said. "Calling all young inventors, that is."

Wendy's eyes sparkled. This was getting better and better. Everyone knew Wendy loved to invent things.

Wendy's room was full of great gadgets she'd made. She had the world's only alarm clock that also poured a glass of water. At least, it did as long as Wendy remembered to fill it.

She also had a walking pencil sharpener made out of an old dinosaur toy. The rubber stegosaurus held a pencil sharpener. When Wendy clapped her hands, it walked from the corner of her desk and stopped under her desk lamp. Her favorite thing to do was build gadgets and make machines. Wendy turned up the volume and stared at the television screen.

On television a reporter stood in front of a strange old house. "Dr. Binsworth, our contest sponsor, would not appear on camera, but he did agree to let us set up our cameras here in front of his house," the reporter said. "The mysterious inventor has announced a very unusual contest. The contest is open to kids 13 and under. Contestants must design and build a go-car, as Dr. Binsworth calls it. It's a car that runs downhill without an engine. Details and rules can be found in today's newspaper. So, kids, get those tools ready! This is Tanya Lopez reporting."

Wendy jumped up and ran to the table in the kitchen, where her father was reading the newspaper. Wendy began jumping up and down in front of him. She waved her arms in the air and asked, "May I please read the newspaper?"

"Since when is the newspaper so important to you?" Mr. Asato said, laughing.

He handed Wendy the paper. She quickly began flipping the pages.

Then she found it. The headline read, "RECLUSIVE INVENTOR SPONSORS GO-CAR CONTEST."

"What does the word *reclusive* mean?" Wendy asked.

Wendy's mom had followed her into the kitchen. She answered, "It means very private, someone who stays to himself."

Wendy's dad read over her shoulder. "I know Bartleby Binsworth," he said. "I've never actually seen him, but he often sends me lists of items he wants delivered to his house." Wendy's dad owned a hardware store in town.

"He does?" Wendy asked, surprised.

"I guess he uses them for his inventions. Last week he bought 400 rubber sink stoppers, a five-pound magnet, and a garden rake! I wonder what he made," Mr. Asato said.

Wendy read the contest rules out loud. "Contestants may work alone or with a group. You must be able to steer and brake the go-car for downhill racing, but it may NOT have a motor. In one month a race will take place to decide the winner. Most important, each go-car has to be made only from . . . JUNK."

"Junk?" Wendy said. The news article went on to say that Dr. Binsworth believed the best inventions were made from surprising things. He was also a big believer in recycling.

Wendy put the paper down and smiled.

"I like this contest," she said. "I've heard about building go-cars out of kits that you buy, but this project calls for real IMAGINATION!"

"Yeah, and lots of junk!" said Andrew. He was one of Wendy's twin brothers, who had just entered the room.

"Yeah, and lots of junk!" said David. He was the other twin.

Wendy laughed. "Do you guys have to say everything twice? Wait! Don't answer that!"

Wendy ran to her room. She couldn't wait to start looking through her tools. She had so many that a whole corner of her room was filled with them, all neatly organized.

She knew she could design and build a go-car for the contest. There was just one thing. She didn't want to do it alone.

Wendy was not reclusive! She liked working with other people on a team. More people meant more energy, more good ideas, and more fun. So Wendy got on the phone and began calling her best friends, Luke Williams, Karen Harper, and Steve Alvarez.

CHAPTER 2

Nuts and Bolts

That weekend, Wendy and her friends had their first planning meeting. Karen brought her notebook to keep track of all the ideas that were discussed in the meeting. Karen enjoyed research and organization.

Luke brought his favorite books about outer space to give the team ideas for what a state of the art, space-age go-car should look like. Luke was a real techie, someone who was always interested in the latest technology.

Steve brought some cookies to help them keep up their strength. "Thinking is hard work," he said. He also brought a book he had about an artist who used stuff he found in junkyards to make beautiful sculptures. "Found art is cool," Steve said, "but it sure would be easier if we could just use a kit."

"I don't agree," Wendy told him. "If we all use kits, all of the go-cars will look the same. This way we have a chance to invent our own go-car, one that'll look the way *we* want it to."

"We'll need some good junk to make a go-car like this," Luke said. He held up a picture of a shiny silver spaceship with big metal wings, flaps, and a rudder. They had all agreed to choose this as their basic design. It looked interesting, and they hoped the wings would help it move faster.

"So let's go out and start looking for junk!" Steve cried.

The kids left Wendy's house and began walking. They were looking for junk. The problem was, there wasn't any junk to find. The city's junk day had been a week ago. Everyone had gotten rid of the junk they didn't want. The kids kept walking until they were near the main street where the stores were.

Wendy said, "In the back of the stores there are big garbage bins. Maybe we can find something there."

They were near Mr. Asato's hardware store, so they headed there first. He was with a customer. They waited until he was free.

"Hello, Wendy, Steve, Karen, and Luke," he said, smiling. "What can I do for you?"

"Can we look through your trash?" Steve blurted. Everyone laughed, including Mr. Asato. Steve blushed until his ears were bright pink.

"That's OK, Steve," Mr. Asato reassured him. "I think I know what you're looking for."

He took them out the back door. Now they were behind the row of stores where the big metal trash bins were. It would have been too dangerous to try to look inside them, but there was lots of junk piled around on the ground.

"Look! We just got lucky!" Wendy called.

She had found some boxes that contained a few nuts and bolts, some nails, and tangled wire. There were gears and little wheels that looked as if they came from a machine. There were lots of strangely shaped pieces of metal and four big metal rods. It was an interesting collection of things for a go-car. Mr. Asato lent them a wheelbarrow to put the boxes in. They took turns pushing it all the way back to Wendy's house.

When they got there, the kids started pulling things out of the boxes. They tried to figure out how they could use the things to make a go-car.

Wendy said, "We found some really good junk we can use for our go-car, but we need to find more. We still need parts to make the actual body of the go-car."

Karen asked, "Where does junk end up?"

Luke snapped his fingers. "That's easy. It goes to a junkyard. Does anyone know where the River City junkyard is?"

"Yes," said Steve, "and I've heard it has all kinds of great stuff. I've also heard some weird stories about it. I heard from some other kids that the man who runs the junkyard caught some kids trying to sneak in. He and his big, mean dog chased them for blocks!"

The kids looked at each other. The junkyard sounded like the best place to find parts. It also sounded a little scary.

CHAPTER 3

The Junkyard

Mr. Asato agreed to go with the kids to the junkyard after he closed the hardware store early at three o'clock. They all met back at the store and got into the Asatos' car.

"There seem to be stories about a lot of people who are a part of this project," Wendy said. "First there are stories about Dr. Binsworth and how he never leaves his house. Now there are rumors about the junkyard man and his dog. I wonder what the truth really is?"

Luke said, "I heard that Dr. Binsworth doesn't like to leave his house because he's scared of people."

"I heard that none of his inventions work right. He stays inside because he's embarrassed by them," added Steve.

Mr. Asato just smiled and shook his head.

The junkyard was on the edge of town near the river. Now the kids could see the fence in the distance. What if all the rumors were true? What if the man who ran the junkyard was mean to them?

As they got closer to the junkyard, the kids could see piles and piles of strange things. There were twisted mounds of metal and stacks of broken wood. There were rusty machine parts, old tires, and torn furniture. There was junk everywhere. Somewhere behind the junk, a dog growled and barked.

After they got out of the car, the kids and Mr. Asato approached the gate to the junkyard. It was shut with a big lock and chain.

"Is anyone there?" Wendy called.

"Who's there?" replied a loud voice.

The kids all jumped. A man with shaggy hair and rumpled work clothes came out. He held a big pipe in his hands.

Mr. Asato nodded encouragingly, so Wendy spoke up first. "We're trying to find parts to build a go-car for Dr. Binsworth's contest. May we please look here?" she asked.

"Well, any friend of Bart Binsworth is a friend of mine," the man said. He put down the pipe and unlocked the gate. Then he whistled. "Here, Snowball! Come meet our new friends, girl." A big black dog came running toward the kids, wagging her tail happily.

"I'm Will Munger," the man said, smiling and shaking hands with Mr. Asato. "Welcome to my place. I call it Will's Wonderland of the Worn But Worthy. Get it? It sounds so much better than junkyard, doesn't it?" Snowball barked as if to say, "You bet!" and sat down.

The kids looked at each other. Now that they could see how nice Will and Snowball were, they felt sort of foolish. The stories weren't true at all.

"We thought . . ." began Luke.

"I know, I know," said Will. "Kids get the wrong idea and instead of finding out the truth, they start stories. There are even stories about Snowball!" He patted the big dog affectionately. "Snowball does a good job as a watchdog," Will went on. "She doesn't let anyone in who doesn't belong here." Snowball barked again.

"As long as you're here on official business, Snowball won't bother you at all. Official business means that you have my permission to look around and take things," Will told them. "Now, I'll show you where you can find some great stuff for your go-car."

They spent the rest of the day looking through all the things Will had. He told them stories about Snowball and about all the funny things people had asked him for over the years. Once Will managed to find a lamp shaped like a big pink pig for a woman. Another time he helped find 50 pounds of old metal spoons for a sculpture a man was making.

"Hey! I've seen a picture of that sculpture in a book," cried Steve. "It is so cool!"

Will told them everything they wanted to know, except he wouldn't tell them anything about Dr. Binsworth. Whenever anyone asked a question about him, Will only said, "You'll just have to see for yourselves someday."

By the end of the day, the kids had an enormous pile of things for their go-car, and they had made a new friend, too. In fact, if they counted Snowball, they had made two new friends that day.

Mr. Asato agreed to come back the next day with his pickup truck to collect some of the bigger items. The rest they piled into the trunk of Mr. Asato's car.

The Flood

For weeks most of the kids in River City were busy building go-cars. Every group had a different idea of what the go-car should look like. It was fun to walk around town and see how different they all were.

Wendy and her friends thought their go-car was the best, of course. The main part of the car was a big tin washtub that had come from Will's Wonderland. It looked fancy, and it was big enough to hold Wendy and her friends. They'd even put together smaller metal scraps to make wings. Luke had hammered out the front so it looked a little like the nose cone of a spaceship.

Karen and Wendy were in charge of steering. Ropes connected the wheel to movable wooden slats positioned at the bottom of the washtub. One was attached to the rudder, which was a flat piece of wood attached to the back of the car to help steer it.

Steve and Luke tried to figure out how to make brakes to slow down the go-car and make it stop. They experimented with different kinds of wheels.

Some of their ideas didn't work, but they didn't give up. They found out that instead of the 16 roller skate wheels they'd wanted to use at first, four larger wheels worked better.

No matter what they tried, though, the go-car was slow. Karen tried attaching a big sail to the back of the car to help it go faster. It just fell down and got tangled in the wheels.

Luke tried attaching wide pipes along the top of the tub. He thought that if air could swish through the holes, it might make the go-car faster. That didn't work either.

Steve tried oiling the wheels so they'd spin faster. Wendy tried angling the wings so they didn't push against the air as the car moved.

Each time they tried something new, it was a little exciting. They never knew what would happen next!

Finally the day of the big race arrived. Everyone brought their go-cars to the parking lot at the bottom of the big hill on Wilson Lane. There the judges would make sure that the cars were all made out of junk and that they all had brakes and some kind of steering device. Then the kids could take their cars to the top of the hill for the race.

Wendy and her friends rolled their go-car into line with all the other cars. Mr. and Mrs. Asato had come with them to watch the race.

They were all very proud of their go-car with its metal wings. It turned out to be the biggest of all the go-cars.

"I just hope it goes fast enough," Wendy murmured. She wanted to win the contest!

Suddenly a police car pulled up with its lights flashing. An officer got out. "Everyone please go home right away," she said. "This area is being evacuated immediately. The river is rising because of a problem at the dam. The water may flood this area. For more information, check your local television and radio stations."

Some kids tried to wheel their go-cars with them as they left, but the police officer stopped them. "My orders are to protect people, not go-cars. Leave your go-cars here for now."

Since their house was closest, the Asatos took Wendy and her friends there. "Please call your parents and tell them where you are," Mr. Asato told everyone. "Then we'll watch the news to see what's going on."

When they'd all settled in front of the television, they saw a special bulletin. Something had happened at the river dam outside of the city. A great deal of water had been released, which was now rushing down the river in a huge wave.

A reporter was standing near the dam. Behind him the kids could see water rushing from a huge pipe.

"The valve that controls this pipe is letting too much water out," the reporter said. "Any minute we expect floodwater to wash down the streets nearest the river. That includes Wilson Lane and the nearby streets. Please stay away from this area until the valve has been fixed and we are sure the water won't rise anymore. An engineer is working on the problem now."

The kids were worried. This flood sounded serious. What would happen to their go-car?

CHAPTER 5

Go-Boat to the Rescue

Everyone watched as the news showed floodwater starting to rise on Wilson Lane. It was a few feet deep before an engineer at the dam was able to repair the valve. The water finally stopped pouring through the pipe, but the water that was flowing toward town would take a while to go down.

Not long afterward, the reporter came back on to say, "The worst of the flood is over. You can go outside, but be careful. It will take a few hours for the floodwater to recede."

"Can we go to Wilson Lane, Dad?" asked Wendy. "We need to check on our go-car!"

"I'll go with you," Mr. Asato said.

It turned out to be a good thing that Wendy's father owned a hardware store. One of the things he sold were big rubber boots. He had a carton of them in the garage. Everyone put on a pair, and Mr. Asato wore his fishing waders. These were a combination of boots and overalls that would keep Mr. Asato dry even in water above his waist.

Within minutes, everyone was ready to go. The go-car was going to be saved!

By the time the kids and Mr. Asato reached Wilson Lane, the water was just under two feet deep. The water had slowed and was now flowing gently down the streets. There were strange things floating past them as they sloshed through the water. The kids saw a broom, children's toys, and plastic lawn furniture float by. They saw a big straw hat and even a flowerpot.

"This must be what a duck feels like," said Wendy, splashing through the deep water. The big rubber boots kept her dry.

All of the go-cars that had been lined up so neatly only two hours before were now a mess. Some were pushed up against bushes and trees. Others were clumped in a banged-up heap that was mostly underwater. Car parts floated in the floodwater.

The kids looked all around. "Where is our go-car?" Wendy asked.

Then Karen yelled, "There it is!"

Far from the other cars, their go-car floated against a tree. Mr. Asato waded over and pulled it back to where the kids were. It had a few dents and scratches, but otherwise it looked great! Its silver wings and hollow metal body helped it stay upright in the water.

"Look!" cried Wendy. "It's as good as any ship at sea!"

"It's a go-*boat*, now!" said Luke.

"Do you think we can get inside and take it for a ride?" Karen asked.

Mr. Asato looked thoughtful. "You can try it as long as you're careful," he finally said.

Mr. Asato held the go-boat so it wouldn't tip over. It sank lower in the water as they all got in, but it was still floating. Inside it was nice and dry, and just a little wobbly.

Wendy grabbed at a tree branch that floated by. "This will make a good pole," she told her friends. "Where the water's not too deep, we can push it against the ground."

It took a little while, but the kids figured out the best way to use the branch to move the go-boat along. They also discovered that their rudder made it easy to steer in the water. Mr. Asato watched them.

They'd been floating along for a few minutes when the kids heard a sound. It sounded like "Meeeeerrrrrooooow!"

They saw an orange-striped cat clinging to a bush, trying to stay out of the water. In the doorway of a nearby house, a girl in a wheelchair sat at the top of her front steps, just above the floodwater.

"Don't worry, Pumpkin!" she called to the cat. She looked very upset.

"Can we help her, Dad?" Wendy called.

"Yes," he called back from the spot where he was standing.

Wendy used the branch to maneuver the go-boat toward the bush while Luke and Steve used the ropes to steer it. Karen reached out, grabbed the cat, and held onto it. Her friends guided the go-boat to the bottom of the steps where the girl sat.

"Thank you so much!" the happy girl told them as she hugged the cat.

"I'll bet lots of people could use our help," Steve said. "If it's OK with your dad, let's look around and see what else the go-boat can do!"

Mr. Asato thought it was great that the kids
wanted to use their go-boat to help people.
Wendy and her friends saved two dogs, another
cat, and a pet iguana. They used the go-boat to
help a man get clothes off his clothesline. They
even rescued one little girl's doll as it floated
down the street.

The go-boat was busy. At each house, Wendy would say "Go-boat's here to help!" There were other boats in the floodwater, too, with firefighters and other rescue workers on board. When they saw the go-boat and its crew, they waved and said hello. The kids were proud to be part of the rescue effort.

Finally the water was going down. The kids got out. Mr. Asato helped them pull the go-boat through the floodwater that was left. They headed back to the Asato's house, pulling the boat. Now the go-boat rolled on its wheels. It was a go-car again.

CHAPTER 6

A Floating Fishbowl

On the way to the Asatos' house, the kids passed Mr. Simon's house. He was a barber in downtown River City, and all the kids knew him. Like Mr. Asato, Mr. Simon was wearing waders. He was standing behind a low brick wall that surrounded his yard. The wooden gate in the wall was closed.

"Why, hello, Sam," Mr. Simon said. He held a long-handled net in one hand and a bucket in the other. "Until I find my fish, I have to keep this floodwater locked in my yard," he said. The wall was holding the water inside.

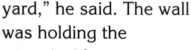

"I had about ten big goldfish in my pond over there," Mr. Simon told them. "When the floodwater overflowed the pond, the fish just swam out onto my lawn. Until I catch the fish, I can't let the water out. These fish have gotten awfully fat since I put them in the pond. I don't think I could fit even one of them inside this little bucket I've got."

"You can use our go-boat," Wendy said. Mr. Asato had looped one of the ropes around the gatepost to keep the go-boat from rolling away. Now he and Mr. Simon pulled it up and lifted it over the wall.

"That just might work," Mr. Simon said. He handed Wendy the bucket. She poured a few buckets of water into the bottom of the go-boat.

"I see one!" Luke cried. Mr. Simon hurried over with his net.

"Got you!" he shouted as he used the net to pull the wriggling fish out of the floodwater. Then he quickly brought the net over to the go-boat and put the fish inside. It swam happily around in the go-boat, which now looked like a big silver fishbowl.

Soon the go-boat was full of goldfish. As Mr. Simon netted the last one, Mr. Asato opened the gate. Water poured into the street and ran along the curb.

By the time Wendy and Steve had pulled the go-boat over to the fish pond, there was hardly any floodwater left in the yard. Mr. Simon carefully netted each fish and put it back in the pond.

"Your go-boat really saved the day," Mr. Simon told them. "Thanks!"

"We had fun helping you," Wendy said, grinning at her father. They all waved goodbye.

By this time, the flood was over. The streets were wet, and there was debris everywhere. The kids were wet and tired but very happy. It felt great to be real rescue workers on an important mission.

They found out from the television news that the go-car race had been postponed until the next Saturday. All the kids would have time to fix their cars that got banged up in the flood.

That night, Wendy lay in bed and thought about the day. Before she fell asleep, she thought, "I'll bet tomorrow there will be more work to do to clean up from the flood. Maybe we can still help."

Racing Fever

All week long the kids of River City worked hard to repair their cars in time for the contest. Up and down the streets of the town, the sounds of hammers and saws could be heard.

Wendy and her friends were busy, too, but they weren't busy repairing their car. They were busy helping their neighbors.

The flood had caused a lot of damage. Many people who lived near Wilson Lane had things ruined by water that had gotten into their basements. Many storeowners had to throw away things that had gotten wet.

This time, Mrs. Asato went with them as Wendy and the kids went from door to door with the go-car, asking if they could help out. Many people recognized them from seeing them during the flood. "Where's that go-boat?" they wanted to know.

Wendy looked at Luke, Karen, and Steve, and shrugged. "Maybe we should just give up and call it a go-boat after all!"

They used the go-boat to move Mrs. Johnson's ruined carpets to the edge of the curb for pickup. They took moldy wooden boards from Mr. Anderson's house to a truck that would carry them to Will's Wonderland. They went to the junkyard the next day with a big pile of metal containers.

"Oh, great!" exclaimed Will. "Bart Binsworth will be happy to have these!"

The kids looked at each other. Dr. Binsworth again! Who was he?

As Saturday approached, racing fever reached a peak. All the go-cars had been fixed, except the go-boat. Wendy and her friends had been too busy helping people recover from the flood to repair it. Its axles and wheels were rusty and creaky from the floodwater. The only thing they had done was paint the name "Go-Boat" in bright red letters on both sides.

The go-boat looked like a rocket but traveled like a turtle! It was slower than ever now. The kids talked it over. Maybe they shouldn't enter the go-boat in the contest.

Karen said, "Last year I saw a television show about a contest to build a machine to sort different-sized balls. Most groups tried to build a machine that would work fast," she went on, "but one group decided to build a machine that was interesting to look at, even if it wasn't as fast as the others."

The kids looked down at the go-boat. "Well, we certainly have an interesting machine," said Wendy. "It's creaky and slow, but it helped a lot of people during the flood. It was a car, then a boat. Now it's a car again, but we call it a boat anyway!"

The kids all started laughing. They wanted the go-boat to be in the contest no matter what!

Left Behind

"On your mark! Get set! GO!"

The first group of go-cars zoomed down the hill on Wilson Lane. Inside the cars, kids wearing bike helmets steered toward the finish line. At the bottom of the hill, people waved and cheered.

The go-cars were fast! They flew down the hill in a blur. Wendy and her friends watched in amazement. At the finish line, judges with stopwatches kept track of each go-car's speed as it crossed the finish line.

There were a few small problems. One car lost a tire halfway down the hill. Big sparks flew out from underneath it as it screeched to a stop. Luckily, nobody was hurt.

Then it was the go-boat's turn. The fastest time to beat was 34 seconds, set by the Saylor twins, Molly and Sam, in their car, "Speed Racerette."

The kids had decided Wendy should be the driver. Entering the contest had been her idea in the first place. She put on her helmet and climbed in.

"Good luck, Wendy! Good luck, Go-Boat!" yelled the kids. Go-Boat was ready to go.

"On your mark!"

Wendy held the steering wheel tightly in her hands. Her feet stayed stamped on the brake, holding the go-boat at the top of the hill until the race started. Her friends had already run down the hill to be near the finish line.

"Get set!"

"GO!"

Wendy lifted her feet off the brake, and Go-Boat started down the hill! The other cars in the line started down, too. The crowd cheered.

Wendy hunched over in Go-Boat. On either
side of her, the other cars started pulling ahead.
They were going faster and faster down the hill.
They were leaving Go-Boat behind!

At the bottom of the hill, Karen, Luke, and
Steve watched the race.

"Oh, no!" said Luke. "I think Go-Boat is in trouble!"

Karen held her breath. Steve closed his eyes. "I don't want to look," he said. "We knew Go-Boat was slow, but this is ridiculous!"

He couldn't resist looking, though, and finally opened his eyes. The kids watched as all the other cars flashed across the finish line.

Way up on the middle of the hill, Go-Boat slowly rattled its way down. The wheels creaked and whined. Inside, Wendy gripped the steering wheel and did her best.

It seemed to take forever, but finally Go-Boat creaked across the finish line. Its time was *twice* as slow as the next slowest entry!

There was a moment of silence after Go-Boat crossed the finish line. Then the crowd began to cheer and laugh. The laughs were friendly, though. The people weren't making fun of Go-Boat, they liked it. Then everyone began to shout, "Go-Boat! Go-Boat!"

Steve, Luke, and Karen began laughing and cheering, too. When Wendy finally rolled to a stop and took off her helmet, she joined in the laughter as well.

"Our trusty old Go-Boat sure did a good job," she said. "It finished the race after all."

Mr. Asato said, "The fans sure like your go-car, I mean, your go-boat. I think they enjoyed getting such a good, long look at it as it came down the hill."

"It was fun!" said Andrew and David together.

A Different Prize

The judges presented prizes to the three fastest cars. Molly and Sam's Speed Racerette, which was made of old boards, won first place.

In second place was Hector Martinez in "Hot Stuff." Hector had used thin metal pipes to make his car. It looked a little like a big birdcage on wheels.

In third place were Jeff Washington and Tanya Polikoff in "The Bamboo Zoom." This car was made from an old bamboo chair and table.

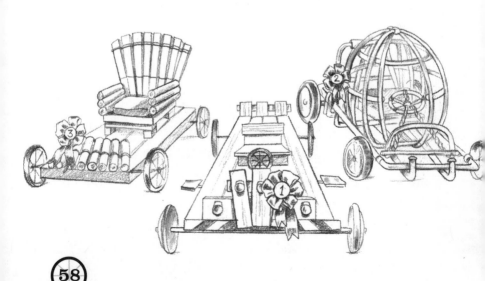

Wendy and her friends clapped along with the rest of the crowd. It was fun to see how many great ideas came out of a bunch of old junk. It was interesting, too, to see how different they all looked.

Then there was an announcement, "Will the designers of entry #32, Go-Boat, please come to the top of the hill with their car?"

The kids looked at each other in surprise. What was this all about? They each grabbed a part of the go-boat and began pulling it back up the hill. Below, the crowd watched curiously. What was going on?

At the top of the hill, the judges stood by a microphone. Next to them was a tall, thin man with a black top hat and a big mustache. The kids brought Go-Boat to a stop next to them.

"Folks, we have a special prize in this contest, and it goes to Go-Boat!" the announcer said. "It's a Good Citizenship Award for all the help Go-Boat and its owners gave to the people in River City during and after the flood last week!"

The crowd went wild! Wendy and the kids looked at each other with open mouths. A special award for Go-Boat was more than they had ever imagined.

The River City Fire and Rescue Chief, Mr. Maloney, gave Wendy a Good Citizenship certificate and then shook hands with Karen, Steve, and Luke. The crowd cheered.

Then Mr. Maloney said, "Now here is the man who saved the town from an even worse flood than we had. He fixed the valve in the dam!"

Mr. Maloney handed the microphone to the tall, thin man with the top hat and mustache. The man spoke. "I am Bartleby Binsworth," he said in a strong voice.

The crowd gasped. At last! The mysterious
Dr. Binsworth had made an appearance. He did
not seem to be afraid of everyone, and he did
not look embarrassed at all. In fact, he looked
pretty happy.

"I believe in recycling, and I believe in helping
others," Dr. Binsworth said. "I am inviting all
the contestants to my house to talk about their
inventions and to see my laboratory. First,
though, I would like Go-Boat
to take one more trip
down the hill."

Wendy and the kids could not believe their ears. Was this the strange Dr. Binsworth who never came out of his house? Was he really inviting them to his house to see how he made his inventions? It was better than great. All those stories had been wrong, just like the ones about Will Munger, the owner of the River City junkyard!

Dr. Binsworth put the microphone down and looked at the kids and at Go-Boat.

The kids looked at each other. Wendy stepped forward. "Um," she said. "Um . . . we just have to know, Dr. Binsworth. Why are you so reclusive?"

"Well, maybe it's because I'm always so involved with my inventions," said Dr. Binsworth, with a twinkle in his eye. "I never have time to spend with people. Running this contest has gotten me out though, and I think I've made some new friends. Now, take Go-Boat on its ride!"

Wendy and her friends hopped into Go-Boat and headed down the hill. This time the crowd didn't stay at the bottom, though. They lined the whole hill and cheered. As Go-Boat wobbled by, hands reached out to give it a little push or pull in the right direction. Go-Boat was traveling faster than it ever had before, all with the help of the people of River City.

Glossary

debris [duh BREE]   the ruined remains of something

engineer [en jun IHR]   a person trained to build and design things, using science

evacuated [ih VA kyuh wayt ud]   left or caused to leave a place, usually for reasons of safety

meteorologist [mee tee uh RAHL uh jihst]   a weather expert

recede [rih SEED]   go back or lower

rudder [RUH der]   a flat piece attached to the rear of a boat and used for steering

rumors [ROO murz]   stories told as news, which may or may not be true

sculptures [SKULP churz]   statues, figures, or other objects shaped of stone, wood, clay, or other material

technology [tek NAH luh jee]   science as it is put to use in making machines

valve [valv]   part of a machine that controls how much of something, like a liquid, flows out of it